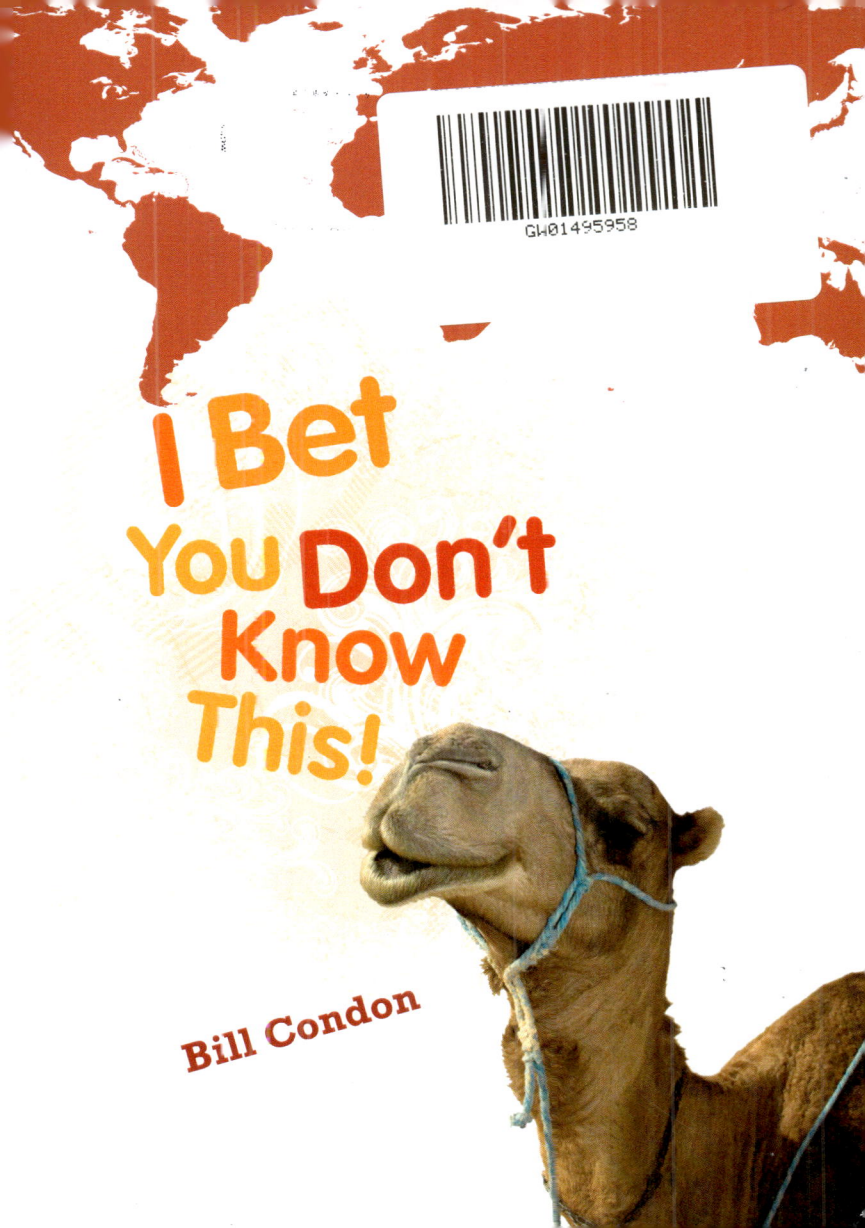
I Bet You Don't Know This!

Bill Condon

Amazing!

Earth is truly amazing, from its deserts with huge sand dunes and underground springs, to waterfalls that plunge from great heights. You can find mountains under oceans, islands that have just appeared and continents that move! And all the time, the centre of Earth is churning with a power that can make the ground tremble and volcanoes erupt! There are so many things to know about our planet that we need to get moving too!

> As you travel through these pages, you'll read about some of Earth's extraordinary natural features. Let's start right now!

Earth has about 70 volcanoes that erupt each year. Volcan Arenal in Costa Rica is constantly rumbling and spewing red-hot lava from its vent.

Explore!

On the Surface

Sitting on plates

PAGES 6 TO 11

Deep Waters

Cool, clear and deep

PAGES 12 TO 19

World of Wonders

Amazing places to go

PAGES 20 TO 21

Hot and Dry

That's some desert!

PAGES 22 TO 25

On Their Own

Island life – what fun!

PAGES 26 TO 29

On the Surface

Earth's surface is divided up into a series of gigantic plates that are over 150 kilometres thick. They fit together like pieces of a jigsaw puzzle. The plates are always moving – but only a few centimetres a year. The movement of the plates makes the earth quake and volcanoes erupt. It builds and destroys mountains and makes and breaks continents!

Major Collision!
The Himalaya Mountains were pushed up when Asia and India collided about 200 million years ago!

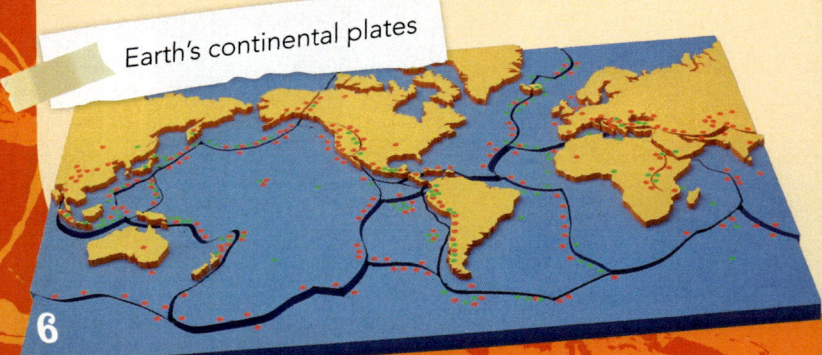

Earth's continental plates

Whose Move?

No one quite knows what moves the plates around Earth, but we do know that earthquakes happen where plates shudder past each other.

When the Europe plate crashed into the Africa plate, the Alps were thrown up. Amazingly, the Alps are still getting higher each year!

Earth is made up of seven continents (or large land masses) that sit on the plates. Asia is the **biggest** continent and has the most people, while Australia is the **smallest** continent and has the fewest people. If you went to Australia you could travel all over the continent and still be in the one country, but if you went to Africa you could visit 47 countries!

Letter Lands
The names of all the continents end with the same letter that they start with – Europe, Asia, Africa, N. America, S. America, Australia, Antarctica!

This is part of Vatican City. Only 940 people live here!

There are 194 countries on Earth. The **smallest** country is the Vatican City State in Rome, Italy. It's less than half a square kilometre in size. The world's **biggest** country is Russia. It's almost twice as big as Canada, the world's next biggest country, and is 69 times the size of the UK! Russia is so big it stretches almost halfway around the planet!

EVEREST IS KNOWN AS THE ROOFTOP OF THE WORLD.

Earth's **highest** mountain is Mount Everest. It's in the Himalaya Mountains on the border of Nepal and Tibet. Everest is 8848 metres high, which makes it nearly seven times higher than Ben Nevis, the highest mountain in the UK. English speakers call the mountain Everest, but the Tibetan people call it *Qomolangma* (pronounced *Chomolangma*), which means 'goddess, mother of the world'.

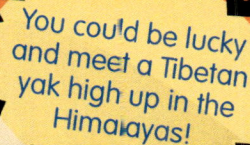

You could be lucky and meet a Tibetan yak high up in the Himalayas!

An Extraordinary Climb!

The youngest person ever to climb to the peak of Mount Everest is Shanbu Tamang. He was sixteen years old when he reached the summit in 1973.

Deep Waters

Oceans cover about two-thirds of Earth's surface and under these oceans are deep-sea trenches, ridges and volcanoes. The Marianas Trench in the Pacific Ocean is the **deepest** part of Earth's oceans, and is the deepest place on Earth itself. If Mount Everest was put inside the trench it would still be covered by two kilometres of water! A deep-sea submarine, the *Trieste*, set a world diving record when it descended to the bottom of the Marianas Trench in 1960.

Inside the **Trieste** were the Swiss scientist, Jacques Piccard, and Lieutenant Donald Walsh of the US Navy.

There's a Red Sea, a Black Sea, a Yellow Sea and a White Sea, but no Green Sea – only a green sea turtle!

P.S. There's a Blue River but no Blue Sea.

> I'm going to be a diver! I've just heard that there is about 200 times more gold in the ocean than has been mined on land in our entire history!

You can't see them, but there are many more mountains under the ocean than there are above! The **longest** mountain range in the world is the Mid-Atlantic range, which runs down the middle of the Atlantic Ocean like a giant letter 'C'. And, would you believe it, one of the world's tallest mountains is mostly under the sea! Two-thirds of Mauna Kea, Hawaii, is under the Pacific Ocean so we can only see the top part of it.

In the Hawaiian language Mauna Kea means 'white mountain'.

The world's largest observatory is on the peak of Mauna Kea.

Fearsome!
Piranhas don't kill their prey first – they just start eating their victim alive!

South America's Amazon River holds more water than the next eight **biggest** rivers on Earth combined! This is because it flows through the Amazon rainforest, which is the largest and wettest rainforest on Earth. When the Amazon floods, it becomes so wide that you can't see the river bank on the other side. And you can't swim across the river either because the piranhas would get you!

Earth would be like the surface of the Moon if there wasn't running water to change its shape. Over millions of years, rivers have carved canyons thousands of metres deep and spread soil over enormous plains. The force of the Colorado River in the USA carved a canyon through solid rock, leaving the Grand Canyon behind.

Snake River
The USA's deepest canyon is Hell's Canyon, which the Snake River carved.

What an Angel!

Angel Falls is named after an American pilot, Jimmy Angel, who landed his plane at the top of the falls in 1937.

This is Angel Falls in Venezuela.

The **highest** waterfall on Earth is Angel Falls in the South American country of Venezuela. The falls plunge off the edge of a 'tepui', or table-top mountain, to the river below. The falls are over 915 metres high. That's as high as a building with 306 storeys! (The UK's tallest building, the Canary Wharf Tower, has 50 storeys.)

If you want to meet poison arrow frogs and three-toed sloths come with me to Angel Falls. I'll introduce you!

The Great Lakes, a group of five large lakes on the Canada-USA border, is the **largest** freshwater system in the world. The lakes are so big that they are sometimes called inland seas. Lake Superior is the largest of the lakes – it is larger than all of Scotland, and has enough water to fill all the other Great Lakes.

This is Lake Superior, on the Canada-USA border. The other Great Lakes are Lake Ontario, Lake Huron, Lake Michigan and Lake Erie.

World of Wonders

Can you guess what place each of these characters is talking about?
(The answers are upside-down.)

I travelled to the largest island in the world!

Greenland

I'm going to see the world's highest waterfall!

Angel Falls

I want to see the world's biggest river!

The Amazon

I've visited the world's largest country!

Russia

I've been down to the deepest part of the ocean!

Marianas Trench

I've climbed the tallest mountain in the world!

Mount Everest

I live on the world's smallest continent!

Australia

Hot and Dry

You might think that a hot and dry desert would not be a great place to live, but almost four million people live in the world's **largest** desert, the Sahara Desert in Africa. About three million people live in areas called oases where there's water from natural springs or underground wells, and where fruits such as dates and figs are grown. The remainder of the people wander the desert travelling from one oasis to the next.

Desert nomads stop at oases to feed and water their camels.

Just in case you wanted to know – the **wettest** place on Earth is Cherrapunji, India.

Drip, Drip
Arica in Chile gets just 0.76 millimetres of rain each year. At that rate it would take a century to fill a coffee cup!

The Atacama Desert in Chile is the **driest** place on Earth. Somehow, more than a million people manage to live there! Parts of the desert haven't had a drop of rain since record keeping began and it has *never* rained in the desert town of Calma. You can also visit places called the Valley of the Moon and the Valley of Death, which didn't get their names for nothing!

If you want to live in a place where it's really hot every day you'll need to move to Dallol in Ethiopia, Africa, which is the warmest place on Earth. It has an average yearly temperature of 34.4 degrees Celsius. The **hottest** temperature ever recorded on Earth was in El Azizia, Libya, where the temperature reached a scorching 57.8 degrees Celsius in 1922. It was certainly extremely hot, but since there were very few weather stations nearby it's likely that there were even hotter spots!

That's Not Hot!
The **coldest** place where people live is Eureka, in Nunavut, Canada. Its average daily temperature is –19.7 degrees Celsius. Brrrr …

Don't forget your sun cream!

WANT TO ESCAPE THE HEAT? GO TO COOBER PEDY, AUSTRALIA, WHERE IT'S SO HOT THAT MANY PEOPLE LIVE IN UNDERGROUND HOUSES!

On Their Own

It's hard to know the exact number of islands there are in the world, but we do know that there are over 2000 islands in the large oceans. The **biggest** island in the world is Greenland and the **smallest** island is Bishop Rock in the UK. And the whole of the UK is ten times smaller than Greenland.

The Newest Island
In 1995, an underwater volcano erupted and formed Earth's newest island, in Tonga in the Pacific Ocean.

This village is in Greenland, the world's biggest island.

One group of islands has completely disappeared. The Aurora Islands, which were once in the South Atlantic Ocean, were last seen in 1856 although they were still on maps until the 1870s. Now people wonder if they ever really existed.

> One in ten people live on an island.

The Aurora Islands may have been near these islands in the South Atlantic Ocean.

The strong and sturdy Shetland ponies come from the Shetland Islands.

If you went to where the Atlantic Ocean meets the North Sea you would find 750 islands off the coast of Scotland. These are the wave-lashed Shetland Islands. These wild, rocky islands are closer to Norway than they are to the Scottish city of Aberdeen! When you go this far north the summer light lasts well into the night. It means that the people enjoy 19 hours of daylight in midsummer. Midwinter is not so great, though, with less then six hours of daylight!

Huge waves crash into stone buildings on the Shetland Islands.

Antarctica is one of the world's seven continents.

Earth's highest mountain is Mount Everest.

The Amazon River is a much smaller river than the River Thames.

The biggest island in the world is Greenland.

The answers to this activity are on page 32.

Now you can check whether you remembered the facts or not!

The world's highest waterfall is Angel Falls.

The Atacama desert is NOT the world's wettest desert.

Antarctica is one of the world's seven continents.

Earth's highest mountain is Mount Everest.

The Amazon River is NOT a much smaller river than the River Thames.

The biggest island in the world is Greenland.